TANTRIC SEX
A LOVERS GUIDE

CHANCELLOR
PRESS

First published in Great Britain in 1997 by Hamlyn.
This edition published in 2000 by Chancellor Press,
an imprint of Bounty Books, a division of
Octopus Publishing Group Ltd,
2—4 Heron Quays, London, E14 4JP

ISBN 0 75370 329 7

A CIP catalogue record of this book is available from the British Library.

Produced by Toppan (HK) Ltd
Printed in China

WARNING: With the prevalence of AIDS and other sexually transmitted diseases,
if you do not practise safe sex you are risking your life and your partner's life.

Contents

Introduction

We are all familiar with sex. It shouts at us from every cinema screen, every newspaper, every glossy magazine. We nearly all indulge in it, and most of us enjoy it. Sex plays an important part in any intimate, loving relationship and, for a great many of us, it is one of the most intense pleasures in life.

Give me, my love, that billing kiss
I taught you one delicious night
When turning epicures in bliss,
We tried inventions of delight.
(T. Moore)

But Tantric sex? What's that? It probably doesn't ring bells with quite so many people. But it's worth finding out what it is, because the chances are that anyone who enjoys sex will find the very real possibility of making a good experience even better.

Western and Eastern attitudes to sex

There is a lot more to sex than most people realize, and the ancient Tantrists held the key to unlocking the possibilities of truly wonderful lovemaking. Even the most unexciting ways of making love, which may have become routine and boring over the years, can give a new thrill when Tantric techniques are applied to them.

In Western society, sex is used mainly as a source of enormous pleasure, as well as for the more practical purpose as a means of procreation. In Eastern cultures, on the other hand, sex has a third purpose. Here, sex is also used as a means of expanding and exploring spirituality, and – by so doing – as a route to enlightenment. This last use of the sexual experience is known in China, quite simply, as a way of *provoking the spirit*.

Tantra is not a particularly easy concept for many Westerners to grasp. It is an ancient body of thought, dating back many thousands of years, and it offers a complete approach to every aspect of living – not simply to sex, though that is what we are mainly concerned with here.

The word 'tantra' comes from the Sanskrit words *tanoti*, meaning 'to expand', and *trayati*, meaning liberation. Tantra is an ancient system of rites and rituals which expands the consciousness and in this way frees us from the constraints of our physical being. To this end, Tantric sex teaches us to use all five senses to their limits and – still more importantly – to push them beyond their limits, thus expanding them through the consciousness of the brain. In this way, Tantra views sexual union as a path to cosmic enlightenment.

Sex is regarded by Tantrists as an entirely natural activity – perhaps the *most* natural of all activities – and, again according to Tantrists, what is natural can never be bad. It is not something we should ever feel guilty about. The only guilt that can reasonably be associated with sex is if you debase or waste your potential for sexual experience.

According to Tantric belief, nothing is forbidden. Everything is allowed. Sexual experience is regarded as a positive opportunity for learning. If it gives you pleasure, it is OK, and good for your well-being, both physical and mental. Sex is an open, exciting and uplifting experience.

Tantrism was not governed by any moral judgements on the rightful place of sex within marriage, or the profanity of sex outside wedlock. However, the benefits of Tantric sex are at their greatest when experienced within a loving relationship.

It is important to point out that Tantra should not be interpreted as a licence for sexual abandon. Far from it. Sexual energy is the most powerful energy that we know, and it is used in Tantra to achieve liberation from the limits of the individual self. It is this liberation that heightens our awareness of the value of each moment and thus allows us to penetrate the spiritual realms of our existence.

The Tantric masters discovered that prolonged sexual union in a loving context produces a heightened sensitivity to the energies in and around them. Rather than turning away from the 'illusions' of physical existence, Tantrists can enter that physical dimension totally and follow in the direction of human perfection to the highest possible levels of ecstasy.

It is possible to redirect that intense sexual energy, which is normally concentrated in the genitals, to the heart and the head, so that a new peak of experience becomes possible. In this way, energy is experienced beyond the boundaries of the body. Thus, sex is the means by which it is possible to achieve the intense joy and inner peace that will transform your life. Through regular sexual experiences, you can become a complete and rounded human being. It is also a natural means by which you can come to experience bliss.

It takes practice, patience and dedication to be Tantric in your view of sexuality. On first acquaintance, Tantra is not an easy concept to grasp. Sex, on the other hand, is. It is a natural source of enormous pleasure for many people.

But that pleasure need not be a purely physical one. It can transcend the physical and become a blissful experience where time and place no longer matter. At its limits, it is possible to feel a oneness with the universe which permits a state of cosmic enlightenment.

Devotees of Tantrism believe that sex means much more than pleasure. It is not only natural – indeed, vital to our very existence – it is also an energy which has as much importance and relevance to our everyday life as do eating and sleeping.

A divine experience

As a result, Tantrists believe that good sex promotes a healthy and happy life at all levels – an experience that may, in fact, be a divine one. They believe, too, that the sexual secrets of the ancient Tantric philosophy can be adapted to our modern lives and applied accordingly.

The result is an entirely new perspective on the art of making love. Sexual energy leads to a liberation from the limits of the individual being. Sex brings with it a capacity for healing, and the potential for a newfound expanded consciousness. The Tantric way is, according to devotees, the path to a longer, happier, wiser, more spiritual life.

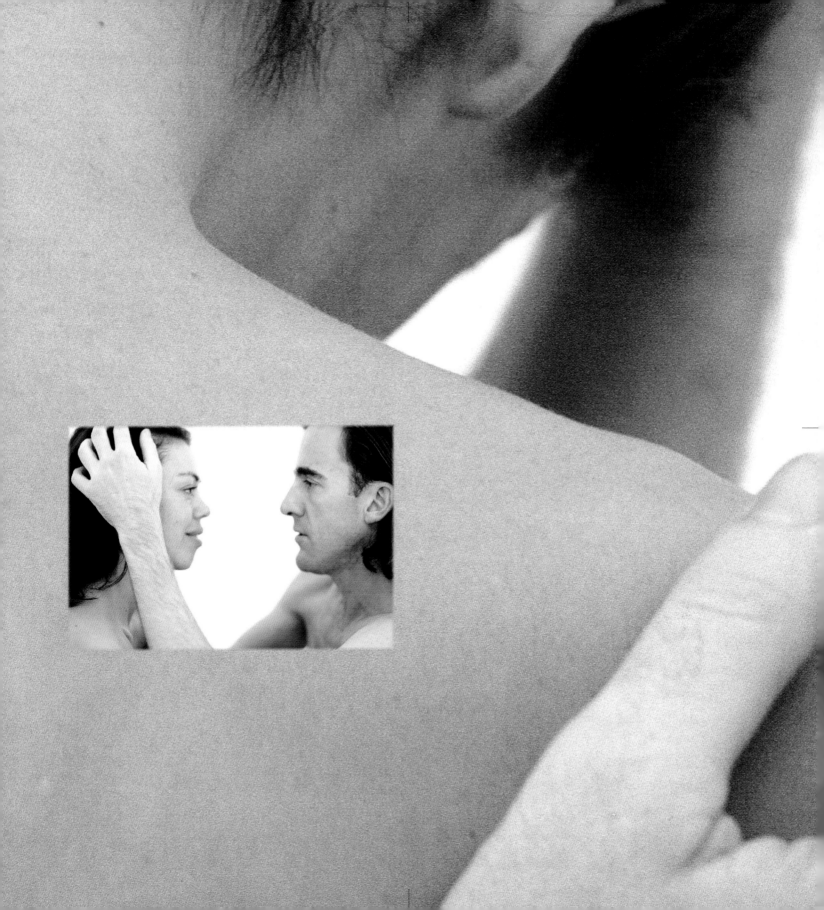

The origins of Tantra

The origins of Tantra have been veiled by the passage of time. It is not known when Tantric teachings first began, but Tantra is thought to have been sending its students into a state of sexual bliss for around 5,000 years. It is believed to have had its roots in India in Hinduism, and then to have spread to Tibet, China, Nepal, Japan and southeast Asia. Tantric symbols can be found in every culture – in Stone Age cave paintings, in ancient Sumerian carvings, in ancient Egyptian texts, in ancient Hebrew writings, in ancient Greek mystical writings, and in Arabian songs of love.

The golden age of Tantra took place during the 11th and 12th centuries, when Tantrism was widely practised throughout India. The Moslem invasion in India in the 13th century, however, caused the slaughter of Tantrists and the destruction of all their manuscripts. This forced the movement to take refuge underground, where it has remained ever since. It had managed to survive in certain remote monasteries, mainly in Tibet, but the recent Communist invasion of Tibet caused a re-run of the 13th-century slaughter and destruction, with another attempt to bring an end to all Tantric practice.

Taoism

No discussion of Tantra is complete without reference to Taoism (pronounced 'Dowism'), not least because of the similarity between the two – and particularly in their approaches to sex.

Taoism is an ancient philosophy from China and is probably one of the very oldest sciences of life. The principle aim of Taoism is for the individual to locate, and maintain, a maximum level of inner energy.

The word *Tao* means 'the way', and refers to the way of the universe. The goal of Taoists is to achieve a state of 'oneness' with the universe. One of the central Taoist tenets is the importance of sex, through which it is possible to achieve a state of harmony, leading to tranquillity and health.

Left Indo-Chinese painting of Shiva executed on a wood panel (500–527 BC).

Right Sixteenth-century painting of legendary founder of Taoism, by Qian Gu.

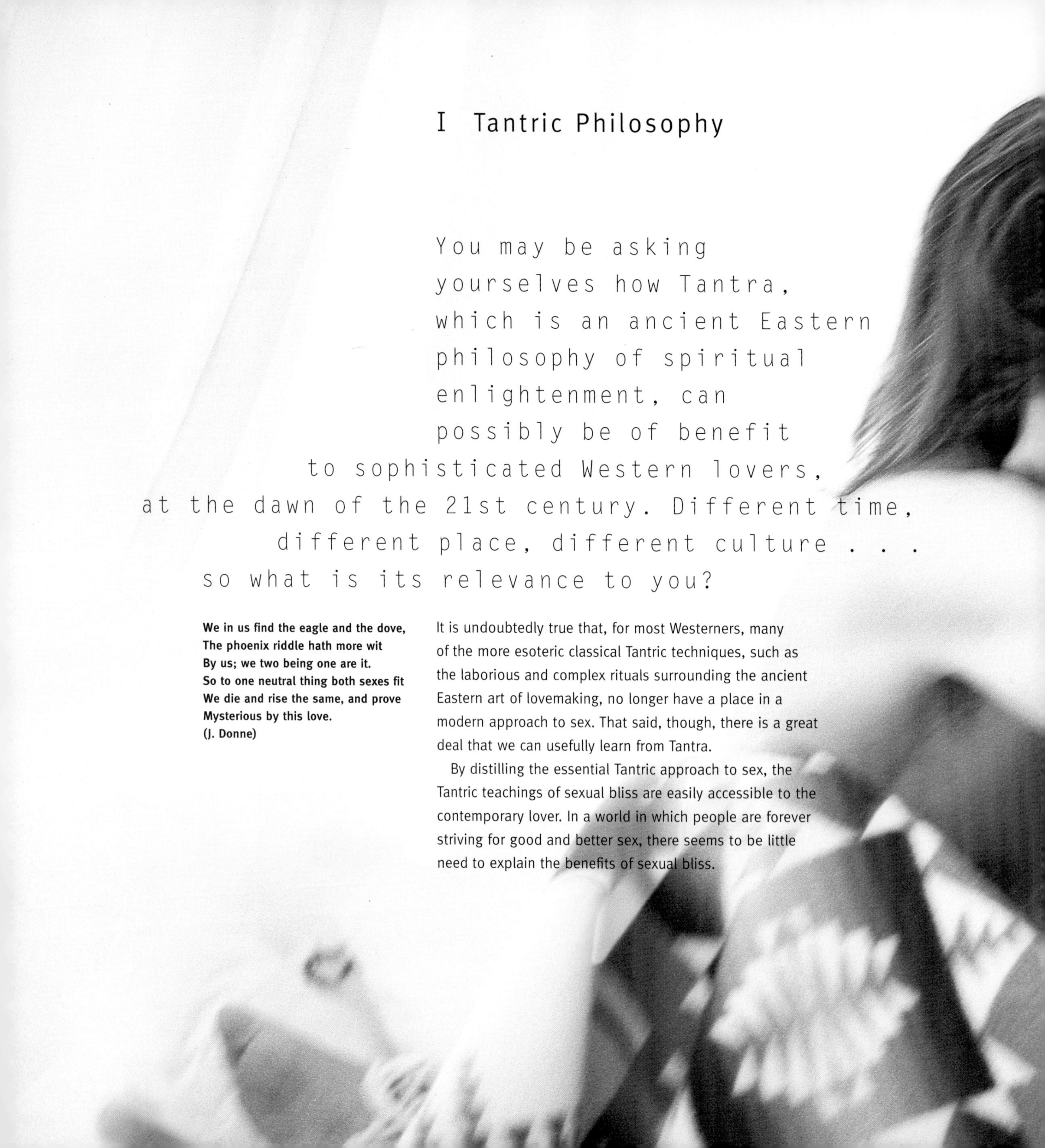

I Tantric Philosophy

You may be asking
yourselves how Tantra,
which is an ancient Eastern
philosophy of spiritual
enlightenment, can
possibly be of benefit
to sophisticated Western lovers,
at the dawn of the 21st century. Different time,
different place, different culture . . .
so what is its relevance to you?

We in us find the eagle and the dove,
The phoenix riddle hath more wit
By us; we two being one are it.
So to one neutral thing both sexes fit
We die and rise the same, and prove
Mysterious by this love.
(J. Donne)

It is undoubtedly true that, for most Westerners, many of the more esoteric classical Tantric techniques, such as the laborious and complex rituals surrounding the ancient Eastern art of lovemaking, no longer have a place in a modern approach to sex. That said, though, there is a great deal that we can usefully learn from Tantra.

By distilling the essential Tantric approach to sex, the Tantric teachings of sexual bliss are easily accessible to the contemporary lover. In a world in which people are forever striving for good and better sex, there seems to be little need to explain the benefits of sexual bliss.

But while sexual bliss may seem to be quite enough for anyone, there is, in fact, more. The ancient Tantrists believed passionately in the healing benefits of ecstatic sex, and modern-day advocates of the Tantric approach are no less convinced. The benefits are numerous and varied, and are surprisingly relevant to many modern-day anxieties. Sexual bliss can ease stress; it can unlock low self-esteem; it can rescue uneasy relationships; and it can even go a long way to saving marriages that hitherto seemed doomed.

Anyone can benefit from the art of Tantric sex: men and women, young and old. All you need is an interest in sex, a spirit of adventure. Try it. It can work wonders.

Where to start

The first thing you must do, before you contemplate doing anything else at all, is to accept responsibility for your own sexual pleasure. This is very important and is the first step on the path towards achieving sexual bliss.

It sounds simple, but a lot of people actually find this surprisingly difficult to do. Still more people have never really thought about it. They have simply made certain assumptions, the most common one being that it is their partner who should assume responsibility for their sexual fulfilment.

This tends to be particularly true for women. If a woman doesn't achieve orgasm, she is all too likely to assume that it must be her partner's 'fault'. But this is not so. It's up to her. The ability to be orgasmic is within every person's own grasp.

So first of all, think positive and do not doubt yourself. After that, be prepared to give yourself both the time and the space to understand what it is you need to do.

Patience

Different people master the art of Tantric sex at different speeds, and some people find it much easier than others. Some people respond to the concept almost instinctively, while for others it takes a giant leap of faith.

On the whole, though, understanding Tantra is not without its difficulties. It involves much more than simply learning something new. It involves challenging beliefs that you have probably held for years, and there are very few people who find that easy. Nothing is more difficult than breaking old habits. But do not allow yourself to be discouraged by your hesitations. Thousands of people have succeeded in moving beyond that stage. You can do it, too.

Energy

Sex is, above all, a question of energy. According to the ancient Indian Tantrists, our sexual energy runs through our bodies like a powerful electric current. This is just as important a part of the human body as the vital organs. Similarly, our sexual energy is meant to be used, just as much as any other component of the human body.

The secrets of sexuality lie in this energy. Finding the key to sexual bliss is simply a question of activating the current. It is very important, in good sex, for each partner to develop an ability to tune in to the energy of the other, and to respond to it accordingly.

According to Tantric belief, it is possible to increase the sexual energy between two people by making contact with certain parts of each other's bodies. Holding hands, for example, or touching mouths, foreheads, stomachs or soles of the feet all generate sexual energy, as does eye contact. Energy can be stimulated still further by placing different parts of the body against each other, such as hands to genitals, mouth to genitals, hands to chest, or feet to chest.

Similarly, there are specific lovemaking positions that are believed to channel energy between partners, which enables them to achieve a feeling of 'oneness', so important in the quest for sexual bliss. These positions are not necessarily complicated, and sometimes all that is required is just a slight adjustment – say, for the hands to join, or for one partner to take hold of the other's feet – to complete the full energy circuit. See also Chapter VII, pages 68–75.

The system of energy centres

According to Tantric belief, the body is a mass of energy centres, or *chakras*, where the body's electricity, or *chi*, is stored. The chakras are depicted as lotus flowers, each petal symbolizing the blossoming of a particular quality or attribute. Each chakra is associated with different psychological or spiritual functions.

There are seven main chakras, running up the vertical line of the body from the perineum to the top of the head. These are, working from the bottom up:

The base or root chakra, which is a powerful source of desire and is associated with sensations of life and survival.

The sacral chakra, which is at the base of the spine and is associated with the sexuality and pleasure.

The solar plexus chakra, which is in the centre of the stomach, just below the navel, and deals with strength, balance, vitality and ambition.

The heart chakra, which is concerned with love.

The throat chakra, which deals with speech and creativity.

The forehead chakra, or third eye, between the brows, which is associated with intuition, perception and imagination. Tantric sex teacher Margo Anand associates this chakra with the feeling a person might have when he or she arrives at the top of a mountain after an arduous climb.

The crown chakra, at the top of the head, which connects us with the rest of the world and is associated with union and wisdom. For people with a well-developed crown chakra, sex is a blissful, mystical experience.

Chakras may be either open or closed. They may be unblocked by activities such as yoga, meditation, dance, listening to music and, above all, sex. Good Tantric sex is all about unblocking the chakras and using the body's sexual energy correctly. Energy runs through the body in a series of complex pathways, or meridians. These pathways are invisible.

The ultimate aim of lovemaking is to awaken the powerful dormant energy known as *kundalini*, which resides in the base of the spine, in the root chakra, and rises up through the chakras. Kundalini is Sanskrit for 'coiled up'. The kundalini is usually depicted as a dormant serpent, usually coiled three and a half times, and sometimes with its tail in its mouth. It is capable of either dreadful destruction or great healing power. As it rises up through the body, it has a cleansing, de-stressing effect.

Embracing opposites

Tantra is a philosophy of wholeness, of 'oneness', in which everything is accepted as an opportunity for learning. One of its central beliefs is that it embraces opposites, which it views not as contradictions, or opposing forces, but as complements.

In this way, male and female are not therefore seen as opposites, set against one another, but are regarded as two polarities that meet in every human being. Everyone, man or woman, is considered to possess both masculine and feminine qualities.

Tantra takes this argument a step further and actually encourages the man to explore his feminine characteristics, and the women to explore her masculine characteristics. Nowhere is this more apparent than in their sexuality.

Thus the male lover is urged to exploit the gentle, receptive, yielding, passive, submissive side of his nature. And likewise, the woman is urged to magnify the strong, dominant, forceful, powerful, dynamic side of hers. The man does not abandon his masculinity, nor does the woman abandon her femininity. They both simply enlarge their potential to include the other end of the polarity. Sexual union is the ultimate union of male and female, and lovers are required to be well versed in both masculine and feminine skills.

In Tantra, the two complementary forces of masculine and feminine are represented by the deities Shiva (male) and his consort Shakti (female), from whose original union sprang the universe. According to the Hindu tradition, Shiva is regarded as reproductive power, and he is often symbolized by a phallus, or *lingam*. Shakti is often symbolized by a vulva, or *yoni*.

Similarly, the Taoists believe that the universe evolved from the harmonious interplay between male and female, known in Tao as Yin and Yang. According to the Taoist tradition, the sexual union of man and woman is symbolized by the union of Yin and Yang, of heaven and earth. Man and woman each represent the qualities of both Yin and Yang, and it is only the predominance of one over the other that decides the sex of the individual.

Taoists believe it is the flow of Yin into Yang, and vice-versa, that allows people to extract the best out of life. The meeting of Yin and Yang occurs as a result of the sexual energy, of *ching*, between men and women, which is tantamount to the life-force.

Yin and Yang are symbolized by a circle divided into two parts with a smoothly curved line which separates the Yin, in black, from the Yang, in white. Each half of the symbol encompasses a dot of its opposing colour, signifying that the two are never entirely separate.

II Preparing the Body

The Tantric masters had great
respect for their bodies –
a respect that many of us have
largely lost today. They
regarded the body as a temple,
a marvellous fusion of matter and spirit, imbued with
a powerful inner wisdom.

Mouth, forehead, eyelids, growing dewy warm
With kisses balmier than half opening buds
Of April and could hear the lips that kissed
Whispering I know not what of wild and sweet.
(A. Lord Tennyson)

This is a far cry from the modern attitude to our
body, whose working we take very much for
granted. We expect it to perform perfectly and
therefore tend to pay it very little attention until
the day it lets us down and ceases to function on
demand. However, the human body is not a
machine – it is a living organism which deserves to
be treated with respect. If it is treated with care,
it will reward us.

Fitness
Most of us lead extremely sedentary lives, sitting
every day for hours on end – at a desk, in the
car or in front of the television. We all know that it
is healthy to be fit but, sadly, that argument is
not always successful in persuading us to improve
our fitness level.

The promise of wonderful sex, on the other hand, may succeed where all other arguments have failed. Good sex requires fit, supple bodies, and for that reason alone it is worth improving your level of overall fitness.

Body awareness

Physical exercise makes us more aware of the body. It helps us understand how the body feels, what gives it good or bad sensations, whether it is comfortable in this or that position, what it is capable of doing.

Awareness of the body is one of the most fundamental requirements for good sex. That may sound obvious, but it is surprising how many people seem to have forgotten even that most basic of principles. Yet body awareness is absolutely essential both for receiving physical pleasure and – perhaps less obviously – for giving pleasure to someone else.

Yoga

Yoga is at the root of much Tantric belief and practice. It is a Sanskrit word meaning 'union' or 'joining', which refers to the union of the individual with the deepest level of consciousness.

Yoga is a system of physical postures, or *asanas*, combined with breath control, which works not only on toning the muscles but also on toning the internal organs. It also enables you to direct your consciousness and your flow of energy inwards, which enables you to 'experience' your body from within.

At its best, yoga fine-tunes the entire body, inside and out, releasing both physical and mental tensions. Yoga is perhaps the supreme exercise in terms of making us more aware of our body and enabling us to feel it from the inside as well as the outside.

In many ways, yoga is therefore the ideal preparation for Tantric sex. It promotes stamina, suppleness and strength, all of which provide a good preparation for many lovemaking positions, particularly the more advanced and complex ones. At the same time, it also allows the mind to remain clear and focused. This is absolutely essential for any form of Tantric practice, in which the consciousness is of paramount importance.

Learning yoga

A few simple yoga postures are shown on the following pages in the hope that they may inspire you.

If you are a novice at yoga, it is a good idea to join a group where you will be taught to do yoga postures correctly. Once you have mastered a certain number of postures, you should be confident enough to practise them at home.

It is best to practise yoga daily, even if only for a few minutes each day. The more regularly you practise your postures, the easier they will become and it is surprising how quickly you will notice an improvement in both stamina and suppleness.

The best time to practise yoga is either first thing in the morning or early in the evening. A lot of devotees find early-morning practice highly effective and say that it makes a positive difference to the day ahead. It is best not to eat for at least two hours before practising yoga, which is another argument in favour of early-morning practice.

Even when yoga has become a regular part of your life at home, you may still like to go to a class. You may enjoy the social aspects of being in a class, as well as benefiting from the help of a teacher who can correct your posture should you make a mistake. You may also welcome the possibility of extending your repertoire of postures.

Practising yoga together, as a couple, can be a lot of fun. It can allow you to get to know not only your own body but each other's bodies, particularly if you practise it naked. It also gives you a tremendous feeling of togetherness, especially if you are close enough to feel each other's breath on the skin and to feel the warmth from each other's bodies. Try to co-ordinate both your movements and your breathing.

Yoga postures

Forward Bend

This exercise stretches the spine (see above). The idea is to bend from the hip. The more you do it, the easier it will become.

1 Stand up straight with your feet hip-width apart and your toes pointing forward. Place your hands on your waist and open out your chest, releasing any tension in the back and shoulders. Inhale deeply and look upwards.

2 Exhale and slowly stretch forwards and down from the waist, allowing your arms to fall gently forward and touch the floor.

3 Hold the position for as long as you can without strain, breathing normally. Lower your body and lengthen your spine a little more with each exhalation.

4 To come out of this posture slowly straighten to a standing position and remain still for a few moments.

Dog Pose

This exercise stretches the legs and renews your energy levels (see right).

1 Kneel on all fours, with hands and knees shoulder-width apart. Curl your toes under and make sure your hands are completely flat. Exhale completely through the nose.

2 Take a breath in and straighten the arms and legs, raising your bottom as high as you can, with your feet on tiptoe. Keeping your legs and spine stretched, lower the heels as far as you can towards the floor. Keep your shoulders down and your neck relaxed. Hold for a few minutes.

3 To come out of this posture, exhale through the nose, bend your knees and sit back on your heels. Rest your forehead on the floor and stretch your arms out in front of you.

Corpse Pose

This is a basic relaxation posture, which will help you relax both mentally and physically (see right). The ideal time for this is after you have practised a daily stretch programme.

1 Lie on your back, making sure you are in a straight line, with your legs bent and your feet flat on the floor. Allow your arms to fall away from your body, palms facing upward. Shoulders and chin should be down, mouth and throat relaxed, and eyes closed.

2 Extend the legs one at a time, without arching the back, and allow the feet to fall apart slightly. Feel the weight of your body sinking into the floor, and breathe gently, allowing the quiet and stillness to permeate your entire body. Each time you breathe out, sink your body further into the floor. The gentle rhythm of your breathing should bring about a deep relaxation, after which you will feel refreshed and rested.

3 To come out of the posture, roll on to one side and use your arms to help you up to a sitting position.

Breathing

Just as yoga makes you aware of your body, so the breathing exercises associated with it make you aware of your breath control. Breath control is so important to Eastern philosophies such as Tantra that there is a branch of yoga, known as Pranayama, that is solely concerned with breathing. Breath control during lovemaking is indeed very important to the success of Tantric sex, as explained in Chapter VII, page 76.

The most basic breathing technique in yoga is that of the complete, or healing, breath. This demonstrates the correct way in which everyone should breathe. The breath itself is divided into three parts: • inhalation • retention • exhalation. You breathe in for a count of one, then hold your breath for a count of four and exhale for a count of two.

The best way to do this is to lie on your back on the floor or on a firm mattress. When you are completely relaxed, place one hand over your tummy so as to feel the movement of air while you breathe.

Exhale any stale air in your lungs, pushing it out through your nose until your lungs are completely empty. Now inhale deeply for a count of one, allowing your tummy to expand. Hold your breath for a count of four. Then exhale slowly for a count of two, allowing your tummy to contract as you empty your lungs.

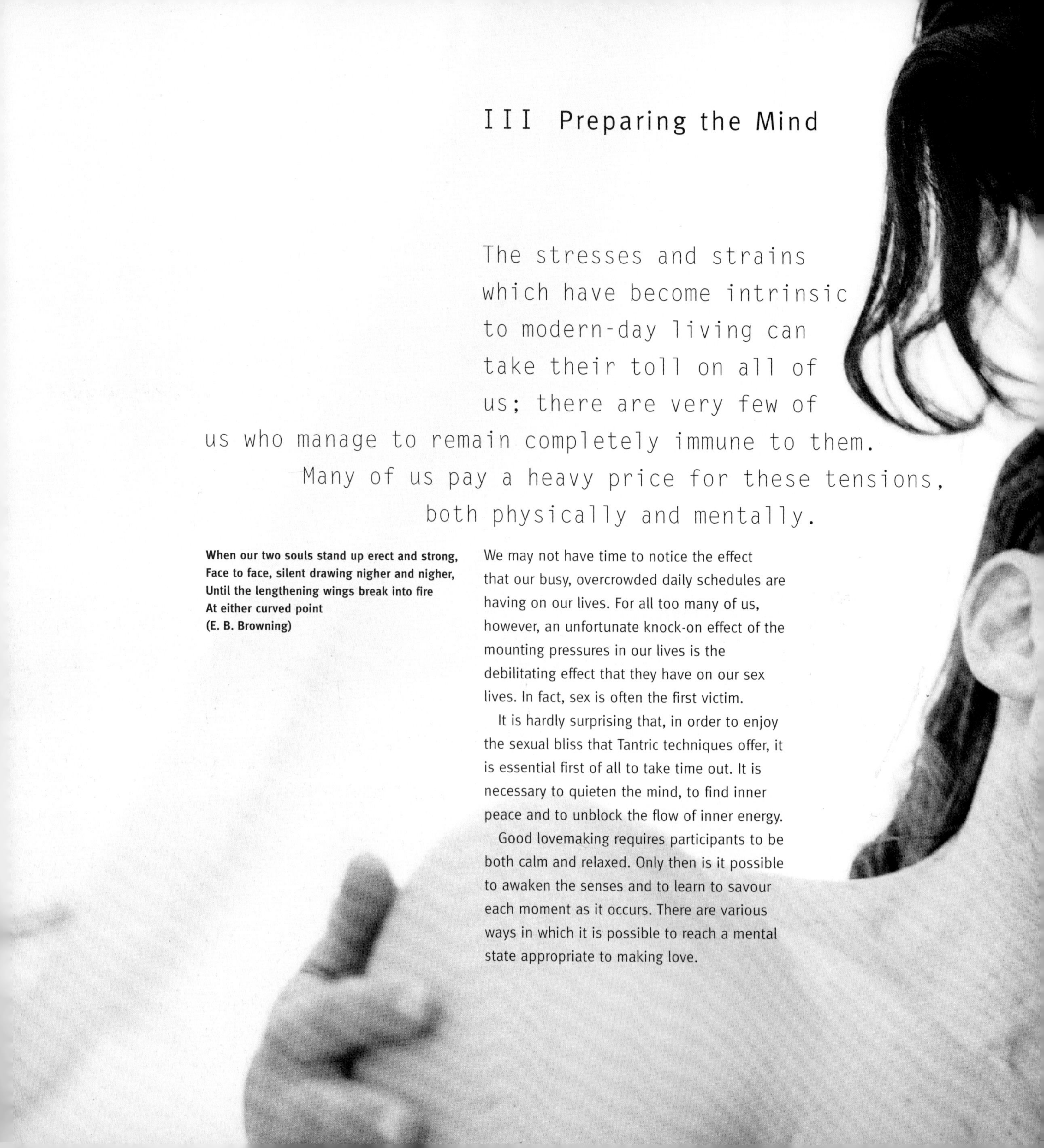

III Preparing the Mind

The stresses and strains
which have become intrinsic
to modern-day living can
take their toll on all of
us; there are very few of
us who manage to remain completely immune to them.
Many of us pay a heavy price for these tensions,
both physically and mentally.

When our two souls stand up erect and strong,
Face to face, silent drawing nigher and nigher,
Until the lengthening wings break into fire
At either curved point
(E. B. Browning)

We may not have time to notice the effect that our busy, overcrowded daily schedules are having on our lives. For all too many of us, however, an unfortunate knock-on effect of the mounting pressures in our lives is the debilitating effect that they have on our sex lives. In fact, sex is often the first victim.

It is hardly surprising that, in order to enjoy the sexual bliss that Tantric techniques offer, it is essential first of all to take time out. It is necessary to quieten the mind, to find inner peace and to unblock the flow of inner energy.

Good lovemaking requires participants to be both calm and relaxed. Only then is it possible to awaken the senses and to learn to savour each moment as it occurs. There are various ways in which it is possible to reach a mental state appropriate to making love.

Relaxation

We all need to develop an effective way of relaxing and coping with the pressures and stresses of life. Different people relax in different ways. Some people are helped by taking regular physical exercise, while others seem to need nothing more than to listen to music, read a book, or collapse in front of the television.

Most of us, however, need rather more than that. We are often a lot more tense than we ourselves realize, and we need to do a little more than just 'take it easy' for a few minutes in order to achieve real relaxation.

Relaxation is a skill. Like any other skill, it has to be learned and then practised until it becomes second nature. One of the most effective ways of relaxing is to practise yoga and breathing exercises. Yoga includes certain postures specifically intended to promote a state of deep relaxation (see page 30).

Meditation and sex

The idea of meditating is that, as a result, you will achieve a certain freedom and clarity of mind. This will enable you to be aware of each and every moment and thus to give it the attention it deserves.

Of course, this applies to everything you do in life – not just to sex. But a heightened state of awareness, and of the relationship between mind and body, will perhaps be of the greatest benefit of all in your sexual relations.

The benefits of meditation

The physiological and psychological benefits of meditation are well documented – it increases the intake of oxygen, it lowers the heart rate, it reduces the temperature of the body, and blood pressure drops – with the result that many doctors now accept that it is a useful technique for combating stress and that more people should include it in their daily routine.

At the very least, meditation gives you an opportunity to devote time to yourself, regardless of external pressures and demands. This allows you to refresh your inner being, which can be, if nothing else, an incredibly soothing, relaxing and revitalizing experience.

But according to Tantric belief, it is also much more than that. It is actually one of the supreme sexual techniques.

Meditation relaxes both the body and the mind, allowing the mind to be still and focused. It lays bare the raw, live, essential person, making it possible to get in touch with your inner self.

This also allows two partners to lay down a direct and meaningful avenue of communication between each other, which no amount of talking could ever hope to achieve. And it stimulates a healthy flow of energy throughout the body, which is such an essential aspect of Tantric sex.

Practising meditation

Techniques for meditation can be taught, but it is not so much about *doing* something as it is about *being* in a certain state. That state cannot be forced. It is something that just happens spontaneously, and only when you are ready for it.

For some people this happens very quickly, for others it may take longer. It does not require any effort, just the right state of mind that is open and ready to receive.

The experience – in other words, what meditation actually *feels* like – varies radically from one person to another. It's a very personal experience, and no two people will ever report exactly the same thing.

Ideally, meditation should be practised daily, for about 20 minutes. Find a warm, comfortable place where you won't be interrupted and take the phone off the hook or put on the answering machine. If you're not alone, tell everyone else in the house what you are doing and ask them to make sure that you are not disturbed.

Meditation techniques

There are several different meditation techniques to choose from. Pick one that you like the sound of and find a class teaching it.

A personal recommendation from someone you know and whose opinion you respect is always the best way of finding a meditation class. Failing that, a nearby yoga centre or health club, or your local library should be able to point you in the right direction.

Different meditation techniques include breathing meditation, transcendental meditation, and watching the sky. Before you start, make sure that you are going to be warm enough, because meditating is known to lower the temperature of the body. You might like to have a blanket nearby in case you find yourself getting cold.

Whichever method you decide to use, the basic technique is much the same. This couldn't be simpler.

Most people sit on the floor, with the legs crossed and the eyes closed. Some people prefer to sit on the edge of a chair, with the feet flat on the floor. Either way, rest your hands on your thighs, with the palms facing upwards, and curl the fingers gently so that thumb and index finger meet loosely on your lap.

Breathing meditation

This is perhaps the simplest of all the various methods that you can use for meditating.

Breathe normally through your nose and focus your mind on the sound and feel of your breath as your abdomen rises and falls. Follow the rhythm of your breathing, and trace the course of your breath with your mind.

If other thoughts enter your mind – and this is quite likely to happen at first before you get used to meditating – simply let them drift in and out. Gently bring the focus back to your breathing pattern.

Don't try too hard to concentrate. There should be no effort involved. With time, meditation will become easy and as straightforward as falling asleep.

When the time is up, simply take a deep breath, open your eyes, stretch and come back gently to your normal state.

Transcendental meditation

This type of meditation is based, in part, on Hindu practice. It was introduced to the West by the Maharishi Mahesh Yogi, and was much publicized by the Beatles in the late 1960s.

Transcendental meditation involves choosing a special word or phrase, known as a *mantra*, to repeat to yourself silently, over and over again. A mantra is a totally meaningless word which is unlikely to distract you. Some people use a familiar name – perhaps their own name, or the name of a pet – but a word or phrase that has absolutely no significance is less likely to distract you from what you are trying to do.

The idea is that, as you repeat it to yourself, your mind will eventually empty and you will find it impossible to think of anything else. This will induce a feeling of relaxation and inner peace.

You may find – particularly when you are new to this – that your mind has wandered and you've stopped chanting the word. If this happens, don't worry. Simply start repeating it to yourself again.

Watching the sky

This is exactly what it says: simply watching the sky. Don't think about it, don't think about whether the sun is shining or it's going to rain – just watch it. It doesn't matter whether it's a clear blue sky, a dull grey one or a stormy one.

As you gaze at it, the idea is to leave everything else behind you until you feel you are part of the sky. When this happens, simply close your eyes and you should still be able to see the sky in your mind's eye.

A variation on this method is to use a candle. Light the candle and place it in front of you. Focus on the candle flame and, when you are ready, you should be able to close your eyes and continue to see the candle in your mind's eye.

IV Promoting Intimacy

There is something ritualistic - almost ceremonial - in the preparations you can make to set the scene. Ritual is an important part of Tantra, helping to make everything about it seem special and important. It helps to amplify the consciousness and to honour both you and your lover in a sacred, almost celebratory way.

How do I love thee? Let me count the ways.
I love thee to the depth and breadth and height
My soul can reach . . .
I love thee to the level of everyday's
Most quiet need by sun and candle-light.
(E. B. Browning)

There are sexual rites and rituals in many ancient traditions, some of which allow you to surrender yourself to the divinity within you. Do your yoga and meditation practice together, then bathe, anoint one another with oils, and massage each other, always doing things in the same ritualistic order. It is not so much a question of what you do, as the intention behind it. The time and concentration that you devote to it are all important.

A bit of preparation in advance almost always pays off. It is not surprising, then, that taking the time to set the scene for sex is important. It evokes the right atmosphere, it creates the right mood, and this, in turn, forges bonds of intimacy.

Different things are helpful in setting the scene for different people, and all are worth trying. Some people respond to visual stimuli, such as lighting and colours, others to atmospheric ones such as music and scents. Broadly speaking, men respond better to visual stimuli and women to atmospheric ones, though this is a generalization and there are no hard and fast rules.

Set some time aside to prepare your space for loving – preferably together. Make sure you won't be disturbed while you're making your preparations, and do this in as slow, deliberate and leisurely a fashion as you can afford. Be imaginative, and share your thoughts with one another.

The very act of setting the scene for your lovemaking will give it a special status. It should become a sexual ritual, which elevates it out of the ordinary.

It is itself a precursor to foreplay, and some people may be surprised by how effective it can be in kindling the flames of passion. Given a little thought and imagination, even a tired old relationship may rediscover how erotic and stimulating the sexual experience can be.

Lighting

It is well known that people differ in how much light they like to be shed on their sexual activity, but coyness has no place here. That said, though, it is quite true that too much light can be distracting and off-putting, while soft lighting is notoriously seductive.

Experiment with different levels of lighting and see which works best for you. Candlelight can be both intimate and erotic, and can help arouse the senses while creating an appropriate backdrop against which it is possible for sexual bliss to occur.

Music

This can be a good time for partners to listen to their favourite music together. You might have quite different tastes in music and you might be able to get closer to one another by really listening to each other's chosen pieces and trying to understand and share what it is that each hears in them.

Try different types of music and see how they affect your mood. Music is very atmospheric and can have a major effect on your energy levels – relaxing, soothing, stimulating and arousing. Experiment and see how it can influence your approach to lovemaking.

Tantric lovemaking, which involves a shift beyond the purely physical into the spiritual realms, demands a total freedom from inhibition and music can help you make that move. Dancing can help, too. You can dance in front of one another, taking it in turns, or you can dance together. Either way, your body movements should channel a strong sexual energy, as well as communicating emotions.

Fragrance

The sense of smell is a powerful aphrodisiac – some argue that it is the most powerful of all. A well-chosen fragrance will play an important part in setting the atmosphere for sex.

Try creating a heady atmosphere by perfuming the room with your favourite incense, or use a room fragrancer and diffuse your chosen essential oils in it. Another simple way of scenting the room is to dilute a few drops of essential oil with water in a plant sprayer, and then spray the room.

Bathing

Taking a bath or shower together and washing each other can be part of your foreplay. It's obviously important to make sure you are really clean and fresh from head to toe before making love, and a clean body, with its own unique scent, is in itself highly alluring. A hot bath will also help soothe any aches and pains.

But bathing together before sex is much more important than the mere act of cleansing. It is part of the sexual ritual, as well as being heavy with symbolism – the cleansing of any bad feelings or negative energy.

Dressing for sex

Lovers in ancient Indian pictures depicting sex are rarely naked. This is not because of prudery, but indicates an awareness of how a partially undressed lover can be more erotic than one who is completely naked.

The Tantrists believed that sex should not only be blissful, it should also be fun, and it is enjoyable to try the same approach. Dressing provocatively for your lover may be frowned on by some people in the West, but there is absolutely nothing wrong with it. The experience of partially dressed sex, and the friction of fabrics, can feel very different. Try making love on black silk sheets for a more sensual and exciting feel. Anything that takes sex out of the boring, the humdrum and the routine has to be a good thing. It revitalizes energies and enthusiasm.

Ancient Tantric practices went even further than simply dressing for sex. They included such activities as ornamenting the face and body, using jewellery, cosmetics and body painting. You might even like to try wearing each other's clothing to see just how it feels to be each other.

Be as imaginative and dramatic as you like, no holds barred, and remember it should be fun. The more daring you are, the more exciting it will be for both of you, awakening both body and mind to new experiences.

Eating and drinking

Contrary to what most people believe in the Western world, according to many Indian sexual texts such as the *Kama Sutra*, the classic Hindu love manual written about 3000 BC by a sage called Vatsayana, sex should not be viewed as a separate activity from the rest of life. Accordingly, there is nothing wrong with indulging any of the other senses during a sexual encounter.

Good food and drink are well-known pleasures which can help to heighten the intensity of any sensual experience. Accordingly, many people find that indulging in their favourite foods and drinks – particularly when a couple do it together – can be, in itself, an aphrodisiac experience.

Take your favourite foods to bed with you, for example, and enjoy them – not as a separate activity but while you are locked in a passionate embrace with your loved one. If this is a messy business, don't worry about it and be sure to keep your sense of humour.

Wholesome, fresh, natural foods help to nourish both the body and the mind, and to increase the levels of energy available to them. Eating food that is as free as possible from chemical additives or residues of pesticides, herbicides and fertilizers is obviously more desirably nutritionally and helps maintain a state of health and balance.

Keep to light meals that won't make you feel bloated or sleepy. There are few things less conducive to sex – good or otherwise! – than feeling stuffed and heavy after a meal.

Touching

Touch is the first language of infancy. Every child knows instinctively how important it is to their sense of security and their well-being. Unfortunately, though, as they grow up, many of them seem to lose their understanding of the power of touch. As a result, people touch each other less and less.

Touch is very intimate, and some people find it difficult to touch others, while others find it even more difficult to receive someone else's touch. Yet touch is one of our most important senses. Touching each other – not just in bed but out of it too – is a powerful means of communication. It is a way of forging strong bonds between people.

Erotic massage

Massage is probably the best loving ritual of all. It is a good means of communication and an ideal prelude to making love. It eases tensions as well as encouraging the free circulation of energy, and a good massage can have psychological as well as physical benefits. It also puts us back in touch both with ourselves and with each other, and it is not unusual for it to give rise to a powerful release of pent-up emotion.

Use a sensuous massage oil, which will allow the hands to glide smoothly over the skin. You can either use a ready-made massage oil, or you can make your own by combining a few drops of your chosen essential oil with a base vegetable oil, such as almond oil.

Anoint each other's bodies with oil and use the touch of your hands both to relax the body and to arouse desire. Take it in turns to massage each other.

Warm the oil a little beforehand by standing the bottle in a bowl of warm water. Also, ensure that your hands are warm. Pour a little of the oil into your hands and rub them together.

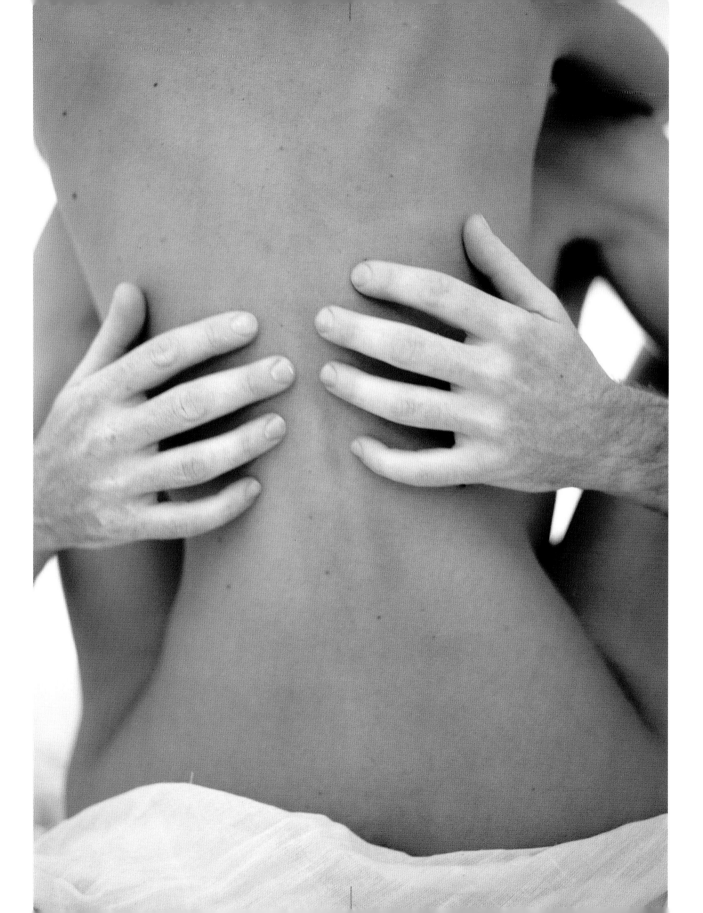

Then spread the oil over the skin. Always keep a hand, or some other part of the body, in contact with the skin, so that you never break contact with the other person. Use a variety of different strokes, keeping them smooth and continuous.

One way of learning enough about massage to make it part of your loving ritual is to invest in a professional massage. Concentrate on the sensations you feel and try to repeat them on your loved one. Supplement what you have learned with your own instincts and feedback from your partner.

The basic massage strokes include:

Effleurage This describes any gentle, sliding, soothing movement. It is done at the beginning and end of the massage, and also between all the individual massage strokes, throughout the massage, to give continuity.

Petrissage Grasp a handful of flesh and squeeze it between your fingers and thumb. As you let go, pick up another handful of flesh with the other hand and repeat.

Percussion This is a stimulating form of massage in which the edges of the hands or the knuckles make small, rapid bouncing movements over the body.

Feathering This is when you brush your fingertips lightly over the skin.

Knuckling This is a firm but gentle pressure of the knuckles on the fleshier parts of the body, such as the buttocks.

Tapotement This is a quick light tapping movement, made either with the fingertips or with lightly clenched fists.

Hacking This is a rhythmic chopping motion made with the edges of the hands, using alternate hands, to tone muscles.

A simple massage

Start with your partner lying face down and spread oil over the back. Work on the upper back, shoulder blades, lower back and buttocks, and on either side of the spine. Then work on each leg and foot.

It is important always to work from the extremities towards the heart, which assists the venous return of blood to the heart, improving a person's cardiovascular tone and general well-being. The exception to this is when you are massaging the head, in which case you should work upwards towards the crown.

Once the person being massaged has turned over, turn your attention to the front, and work on the arms, hands, chest, abdomen, legs, scalp and face.

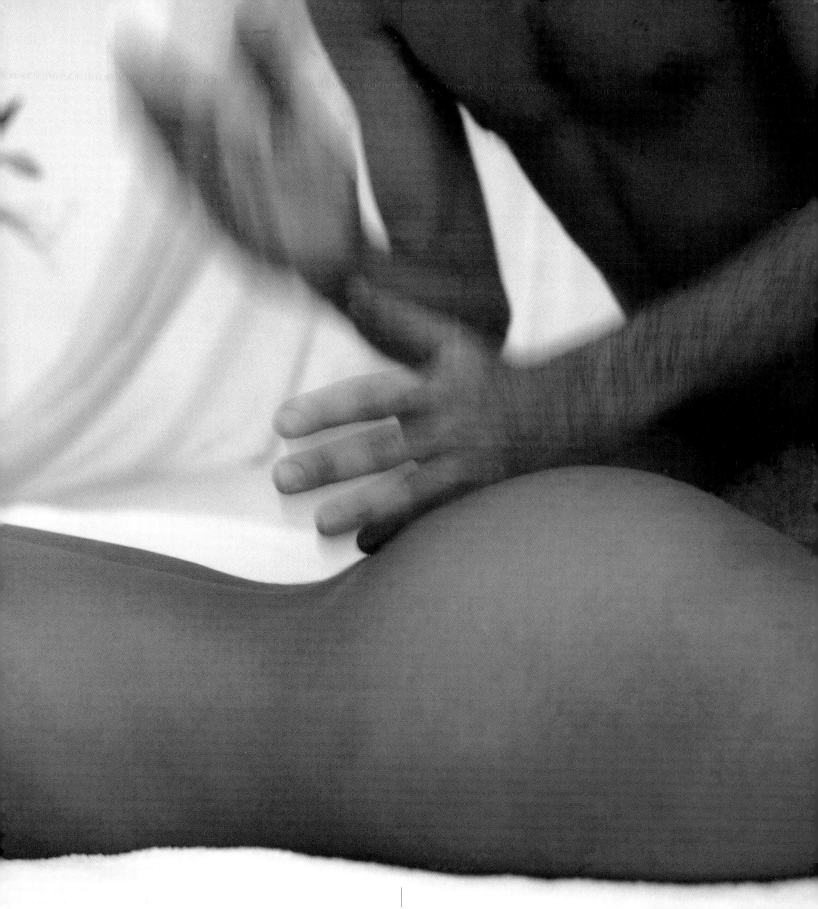

V Giving Yourself Pleasure

No one can deny that the human body is a truly remarkable thing, and in no context is this more apparent than in that of sexuality. Since ancient times the capacity of the human body for giving and receiving physical pleasure has been a subject of wonder and intrigue.

Bring in thy oily streams
The milk and honey age
Now close the world-round sphere of bliss
And fill it with a heavenly kiss.
(G. Chapman)

Get to know your body

The best way of getting to know your body is to carefully examine it, naked, in the mirror. Get to know it intimately and reinforce your positive feelings about it – notice what you like about it and appreciate it for what it is.

Study, too, your genital anatomy in a mirror, and note the changes that it undergoes during sexual arousal and orgasm while you masturbate.

Masturbation

It is virtually impossible to master the art of blissful Tantric sex unless you are intimately familiar with your own body (your partner's too, of course, but that's another story!). And there is no better way of getting to know your own body than through masturbation.

Sad to say, the subject of masturbation still invites censure from certain people – sad because negative attitudes to masturbation deny a person's right to sexual pleasure long after people believe that they have become sexually liberated.

In the eyes of the ancient Tantrics, on the other hand, masturbation was simply another natural aspect of a person's sexuality. Pleasure is always positive, and anything that gives you pleasure is allowed. Oriental pictures of people – particularly women – enjoying self love were very common.

It is only by getting to know your own body that you can understand exactly what you find most pleasurable, and it is only when you know what you find most pleasurable that you can improve the quality of your orgasm.

Once you know exactly what most turns you on, you are then in an excellent position to convey this to someone else and to convey to them how to do it to you, too. In this way, you will learn that *you* – no one else – are the source of your own pleasure. *You* are in control. Showing someone else how you give yourself pleasure is an incredibly empowering act.

Another advantage of masturbation is that it is likely to improve your relationship with your partner. You will understand that you are not dependent on him for your pleasure, and he, in turn, will not need to feel responsible for your pleasure. This removes a lot of pressure and puts both partners on an equal footing.

Masturbation often engenders feelings of guilt in some people, but these are quite inappropriate and have no place here. There's nothing wrong with giving yourself pleasure. In any case, you're not alone – in recent surveys, over 90 per cent of men and over 80 per cent of women have admitted to enjoying masturbation.

For a woman

Spread your legs in front of a mirror and look at your genitals. If you haven't done it before, this can be very revealing.

Cover your body with massage oil and stroke your whole body sensuously, looking for areas that give you extreme pleasure. Some of these areas may come as a surprise – the inner thighs and the inner arms, for example.

Don't concentrate solely on the genital area. According to Tantric belief, the entire body is an erogenous zone and any part of it can trigger sexual arousal when it is stimulated.

Then turn your attention to your genitals. Tease yourself slowly and touch yourself over your entire genital area, perineum and anus. Lubricate the vagina and caress both the opening to the vagina and the inside.

Experiment with different degrees of pressure – light and hard – and seek out the most sensitive part of the clitoris. Do you like an up-and-down movement, a sideways movement, or a circular movement? When you find the movement you prefer, maintain this in a steady rhythmic pattern.

As you bring yourself to orgasm, keep your tongue touching the roof of your mouth. This completes the cycle of sexual energy. As you reach orgasm, you should concentrate on the forehead chakra – also known as the third eye – which is the space between your eyes and slightly above them on the forehead. This pulls the energy upwards, up the spine, through all the chakras and to the top of your head. This may seem strange, but it is an ancient Tantric practice thought to be an act of intense spirituality and to bring about an expansion of consciousness.

Pelvic floor muscles

As your arousal builds up, start tensing your pelvic floor muscles in a rhythmic pumping movement. These are the muscles that you use when you need to urinate but are trying to hold back. Tensing these muscles helps to intensify your arousal by improving blood flow, increasing sensitivity in the whole area including the vagina and clitoris.

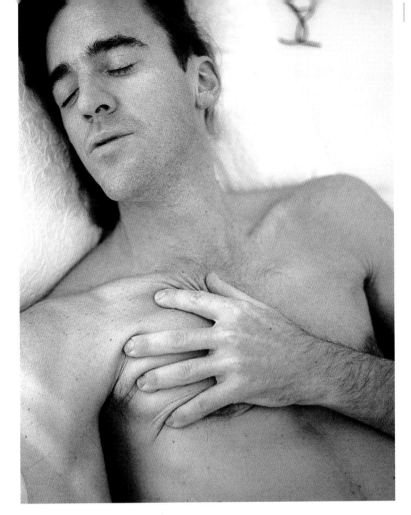

For a man

Spread your legs in front of a mirror and look at your genitals. Cover your body with massage oil and stroke your whole body sensuously, looking for the areas that give you the most pleasure. Some of these parts of the body, such as the nipples, inner thighs and inner arms, may actually surprise you, particularly if you have never done this before.

Don't concentrate solely on the genital area. Remember that, according to Tantric belief, the whole body is one big erogenous zone and that arousal of any part of it can provoke sexual stimulation.

Now turn your attention to your genitals and concentrate on this part of your body. Tease yourself slowly and lubricate your genital area, including the scrotum, perineum and anus. Caress the entire area, experimenting with different kinds of touch, different movements, and different degrees of pressure. Apply firm, steady pressure to the perineum, beneath which lies the prostate gland, inside the body. Massaging the prostate greatly increases sexual arousal and this should be highly pleasurable.

When you feel you are approaching orgasm, relax the genital muscles and keep your tongue touching the roof of your mouth. This completes the cycle of sexual energy.

You should also concentrate on the forehead chakra, which is the space between your eyes and slightly above them on the forehead. This pulls the energy upwards, up the spine, through all the chakras and to the top of your head. This is an ancient Tantric practice, thought to encourage the expansion of the consciousness.

Pelvic floor muscles

Women are not the only ones who benefit from toning their pelvic floor muscles. Men, too, can improve their general genital fitness. Do this by tensing your thighs, buttocks and abdomen for as long as possible before eventually relaxing them. When you have become used to the exercise, you should be able to do this for about five minutes at a time.

Learning to tense and relax the muscles repeatedly in a pumping action will also help you practise semen retention, which is a central maxim in Tantric sex (see page 82), and enables you to prevent ejaculation when you are about to have an orgasm.

Giving yourself pleasure in front of your partner

Having learned the art of self pleasuring on your own, the next stage is to do it in front of your partner. Many people may be appalled at this suggestion. What, me, masturbate in front of my lover? you may ask – never!

But try it. It is a very loving thing to do. In this way, you are sharing your most private, intimate sexual behaviour with your partner. This is a means of establishing a new and meaningful dialogue with your partner, and is the best way of showing her what pleases you.

Set the scene much as you would for making love (see Chapter IV), and sit opposite each other. Then take it in turns to show each other your genital area and how you like it to be caressed. Alternatively you may prefer to do this together. In this way, you are both in the same position, doing the same thing, and no one person is on display. This should reduce any feeling of pressure.

Giving each other pleasure

Finally, you can progress to the last stage, which is when each partner takes it in turn to give pleasure to the other one. For many people, this is the most difficult thing to do, because it means an abdication of control, but it is worth doing not only for practical reasons – your partner will achieve a better understanding of what gives you pleasure – but also because it creates a strong bond of intimacy.

The idea is to follow the same strokes and touches that you saw your partner practise on herself. Remember the movements that your partner used to please herself, and try to apply them in the same way.

Don't worry if you don't get everything right first time, and be prepared to accept some degree of trial and error. When something feels right, carry on doing it for a while. Don't change your movements too soon.

Your partner should be prepared to help you. There are a number of ways in which he can do this. He can, quite simply, say what he thinks; or make appreciative noises to indicate that what you are doing feels good; or change position slightly when appropriate; or move your hand to a more effective position. And you, in turn, must always take notice of what your partner tells you.

VI Foreplay

So far, we have discussed the importance of all the other preliminaries to lovemaking - preparing your mind and your body, promoting intimacy between you, and teaching your partner how best to give you pleasure. Now we've reached the point at which to consider the act of lovemaking itself.

From the soft sliding of hands over me, and the thrusting of fingers through my hair and beard;
From the long sustained kiss upon the mouth and bosom
. . . From the cling of the trembling arm,
From the bending curve and the clinch
(W. Whitman)

Good lovemaking should never be rushed, and both partners should be absolutely ready for it, both physically and mentally. One of the soundest ways of ensuring that both partners are completely ready is with sensitive and imaginative foreplay, which is a vital component of the ritualistic preparation for good sex, itself so important to Tantra.

Arousal

Foreplay is important for both sexual partners. It is important for a man because it ensures that he achieves a firm erection, which is, of course, necessary for intercourse.

It is even more important for women, who generally take longer to become aroused than men. It is only when a woman is aroused that her vaginal secretions will flow abundantly and she will be ready for penetration. Forcing intercourse before she is ready can be painful for both partners.

An understanding of the importance of foreplay – particularly for women – was not confined to Tantric belief. According to Mohammed, the founder of Islam on the Arabian peninsula in the seventh century, denying a woman sufficient foreplay was a form of cruelty.

Western and Eastern attitudes to foreplay are very different. In the West, foreplay is seen as a preliminary to intercourse, and is all too often rushed. In the East, on the other hand, it is viewed as an important part of the whole sexual experience in itself, and need not necessarily end in intercourse.

Remember that, according to Tantra, the whole body is an erogenous zone, not just the genitals.

To arouse a woman

A woman will respond best to a full and gradual sequence of foreplay, which may take as long as 20 minutes or even more.

Start by caressing her head and face. Slowly work down her neck and shoulders until you reach her breasts. Stroking, kissing and sucking the breasts and nipples is an effective way of arousing most women, and can – in some women – bring about a very high level of excitement indeed.

Use different parts of your body to stimulate different areas of hers, and enjoy the sensations of full body contact. Try to touch as many parts of her body with as many parts of yours as possible. Work your way down her abdomen and then concentrate on each foot and leg and work up until you reach the genitals. Caress her clitoris and vulva both manually and orally.

Watch her reactions carefully and try to respond to them as closely as possible.

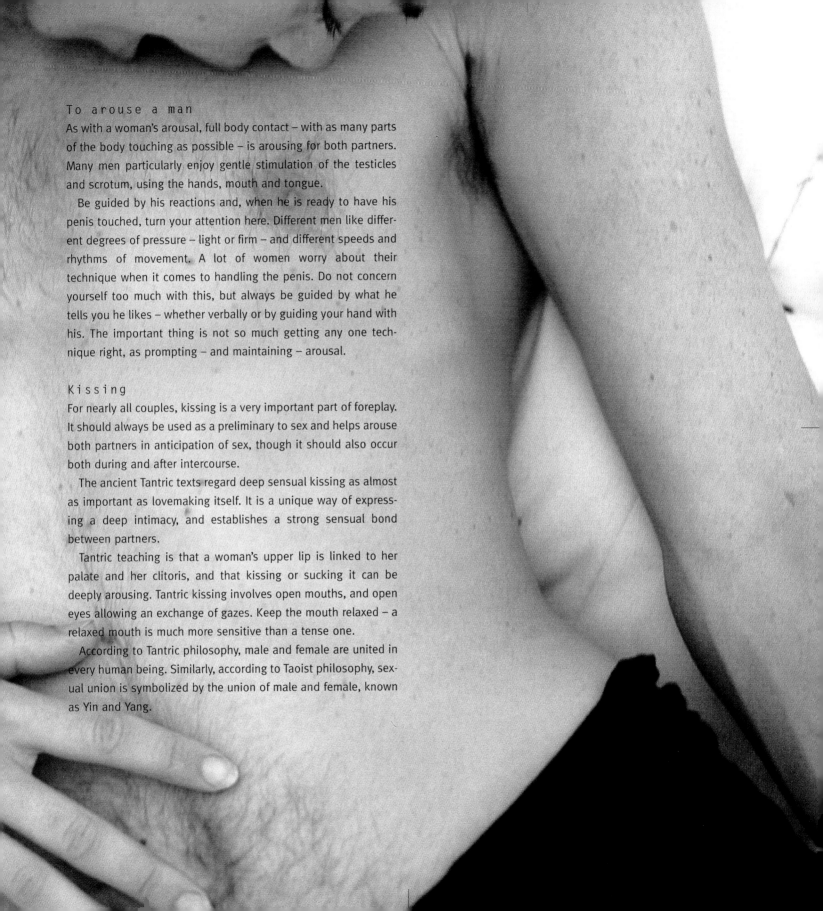

To arouse a man

As with a woman's arousal, full body contact – with as many parts of the body touching as possible – is arousing for both partners. Many men particularly enjoy gentle stimulation of the testicles and scrotum, using the hands, mouth and tongue.

Be guided by his reactions and, when he is ready to have his penis touched, turn your attention here. Different men like different degrees of pressure – light or firm – and different speeds and rhythms of movement. A lot of women worry about their technique when it comes to handling the penis. Do not concern yourself too much with this, but always be guided by what he tells you he likes – whether verbally or by guiding your hand with his. The important thing is not so much getting any one technique right, as prompting – and maintaining – arousal.

Kissing

For nearly all couples, kissing is a very important part of foreplay. It should always be used as a preliminary to sex and helps arouse both partners in anticipation of sex, though it should also occur both during and after intercourse.

The ancient Tantric texts regard deep sensual kissing as almost as important as lovemaking itself. It is a unique way of expressing a deep intimacy, and establishes a strong sensual bond between partners.

Tantric teaching is that a woman's upper lip is linked to her palate and her clitoris, and that kissing or sucking it can be deeply arousing. Tantric kissing involves open mouths, and open eyes allowing an exchange of gazes. Keep the mouth relaxed – a relaxed mouth is much more sensitive than a tense one.

According to Tantric philosophy, male and female are united in every human being. Similarly, according to Taoist philosophy, sexual union is symbolized by the union of male and female, known as Yin and Yang.

Kissing is regarded as symbolizing the harmonious union of male and female. The tongue is considered male – representing the penis – while the lips are considered female – symbolizing the vulva. The mucous membrane of the lips has a similar texture to that of the vulva. Oral hygiene is obviously considered important for harmonious kissing.

The tongue is a highly sensitive organ and is capable of both giving and receiving extreme pleasure. Use it to explore your lover's lips, mouth, tongue and teeth. Use it, too, to explore every part of her face and body. Employ different rhythms and pressures on different parts of the body, including the forehead, eyes, cheeks, throat, nipples, thighs, arms, navel and genital area. Kisses in the region of any of the seven chakras (see page 19) channel energies.

According to the *Kama Sutra* there several different types of kiss. There is the Greatly Pressed Kiss, which is when the lower lip of one partner is pressed and licked with the tongue of the other. There is the Kiss of the Upper Lip, which is when the man kisses the woman's upper lip while she kisses his lower lip. There is the Clasping Kiss, which is when one partner takes both her partner's lips between her own. And there is the Fighting of the Tongue, which is when one partner touches the teeth and palate of the other with their tongue.

Use your other senses as well – particularly those of smell and hearing – to detect your partner's state of arousal. As a person reaches a state of arousal, their body scent changes and they are likely to make tiny, almost inaudible sounds. Learn to recognize these all-important changes in smell and sound, and understand what they mean.

The exchange of body fluids during lovemaking is thought, according to Tantric belief, to be a nourishing and revitalizing process. The saliva is considered to be the most precious of all. Thus you can suck your partner's tongue and even exchange saliva. Tasting your partner's saliva requires love, trust and respect, but once you have done it you are almost certain to want to do it again.

A sexually aroused woman's saliva, which is known as Jade Fluid, is believed to be particularly beneficial to a man's health and strength. Recommended Tantric practice is for the woman to touch the roof of her mouth with the tip of her tongue as she nears orgasm. As she reaches orgasm, she should offer her tongue to her partner for him to suck her saliva.

Oral sex

Kissing, licking and sucking the genitals is one of the most arousing ways of making love. It is an intimate thing to do and an effective way of sharing energies.

The tongue is an excellent source of pleasure – it is moist and warm, it is strong and agile, and it can change its size and shape according to what is required of it.

It goes without saying that oral and genital hygiene should, of course, be impeccable.

Fellatio

Oral sex for men is called fellatio. There are many different ways of performing this, depending on whether the mouth is open or closed, on how wet or dry the mouth is, and on how deep the penis is put into the mouth. Use a variety of different touches and movements, and ask what he likes best.

Cunnilingus

Oral sex for women is called cunnilingus. The ancient Eastern traditions regard the vulva as the most sacred part of a woman's body. It is the Gateway to Life – the passage through which we all pass when we are born – and therefore a symbol of the very source of life. Performing cunnilingus is therefore an act of honour to this sacred centre.

Kiss and lick her pubic mound, and then the outer lips of her vagina. The area known as the perineum, between her vulva and her anus, is rich in nerve endings and is therefore highly sensitive. Lick up and down the perineum, then turn your attention to her vulva.

Kiss the outer lips, running your tongue both along and between them. As you do this, you can also probe your tongue inside her vagina, varying how deep or shallow, slow or fast your movements are.

But the core of a woman's sexuality is probably her clitoris, and most women are highly stimulated by having it licked and probed with the tongue. Flick the tongue from one side to the other, as well as up and down along the shaft of the clitoris. Lick the head of the clitoris, and gently suck this between your lips.

Clitoral stimulation of this kind will usually bring a woman to orgasm. Even women who have difficulty in reaching orgasm often find that oral sex does the trick.

Performing oral sex together or separately?

Some people like to give and receive oral sex together in what is usually known as the '69' position. Some people, on the other hand, find it quite hard to do both at the same time. They find that it means they do both less well than they might, and therefore prefer to do each separately.

Another possibility is for both partners to adopt the '69' position, but then to enjoy oral sex alternately. Think about what you can feel with your eyes closed, where your sexual energy is coming from, and what colours you can see in your mind's eye.

Yet another Tantric practice is for both partners to adopt the '69' position, but then – instead of practising oral sex – each partner should place their own tongue on the other's perineum. This is where the base or root chakra is (see page 19). It is also where the kundalini energy lies dormant when it is at rest. When you have your tongue on your lover's perineum, you should be able to feel the energy begin to uncoil.

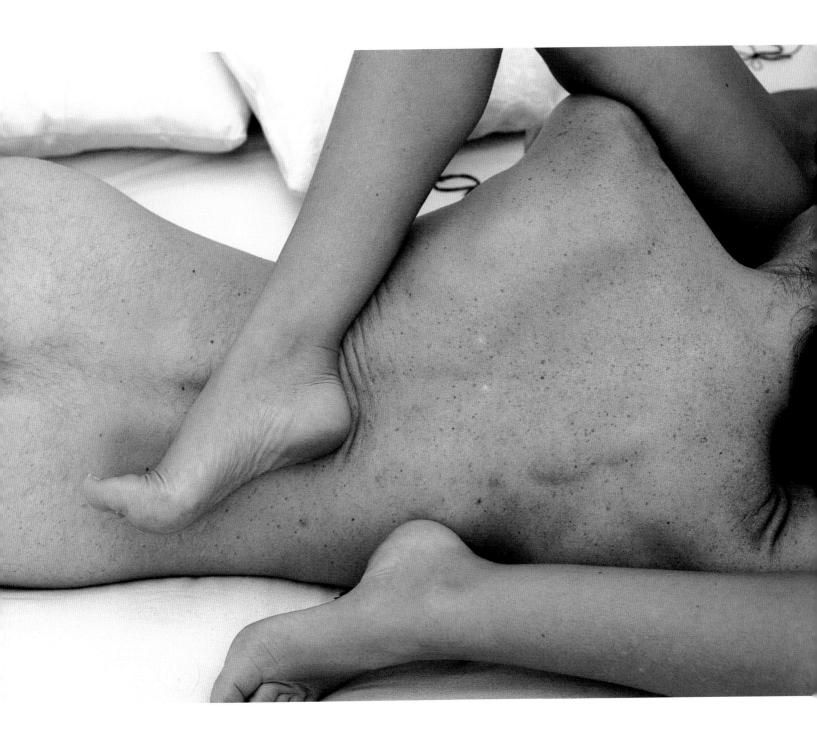

VII Lovemaking

Making love is one of life's greatest experiences. In order to exploit its full potential and to make it a truly wonderful sensual experience, it demands your close awareness. That doesn't mean you have to think too hard about it, though. You don't.

**When I do come she will speak not, she will stand
Either hand,
On my shoulder, give her eyes the first embrace
Of my face,
Ere we rush, ere we extinguish sight and speech
Each on each.
(R. Browning)**

Too much effort would, in fact, interfere with your sensations and detract from your feelings of pleasure. You need, rather, to switch off and relax. The yoga and meditation practices that you read about previously will help you to do this.

Positions

Everyone has their favourite positions for lovemaking. That said, though, it is important not to become stuck in your ways and trapped in a rut. You must always try to remain open to new and exciting possibilities.

Tantra encourages all kinds of experimentation and variety, and nowhere is this truer than in the realm of sex. Trying new positions helps to focus the mind on the sexual act.

Moving from one position to another – perhaps several times – during one lovemaking session can be very pleasurable. If you want to do this, communicate your wishes to your partner, either with speech or gestures. This kind of intimate communication is an important part of a sexual relationship.

Much of the ancient erotic art of the East depicts Tantric lovers who are highly skilled at using their bodies to create the most complex, beautiful shapes and patterns. Many of these Eastern lovemaking positions are described in the *Kama Sutra*, which is perhaps the most famous sex manual of all time.

According to the *Kama Sutra*, there are only a few basic sex positions. These are man on top, woman on top, and rear entry. Any other positions are only variations on these three basic ones. They may be simple or complex, straightforward or adventurous, easy to follow or gymnastic.

Man on top

Man-on-top, or *Uttana-bandha*, positions give the man control over the pace, depth, intensity and intimacy of intercourse. They allow full eye contact, which is important in Tantric sex, and there is plenty of scope for kissing each other on the mouth.

The best known man-on-top position is the missionary position, known in Eastern practice as the Yawning Position. The woman lies on her back with her legs wide open.

There are many variations on this basic position, depending on what the woman does with her legs. If she pulls her knees up against her stomach, this is known as the Crab Position. If she pulls her knees up tightly to her chest, this is the Position of the Wife of Indra. If she wraps her legs round her partner's back, this is known as the Clasping Position.

If both partners keep their legs straight, with one partner pressing their legs firmly along the outside of the other's, this is known as the Pressing Position. And if the man lies facing his partner's feet, this is known as the Turning Position.

Woman on top

Woman-on-top, or *Purushayita-bandha*, positions allow the woman complete control of the depth of penetration. As with man-on-top positions, there is great potential for eye contact and kissing. Many women enjoy this, as they can dictate the pace of the lovemaking. Many men also enjoy these positions because they appreciate taking the role of the passive partner for a while. Another advantage of these positions is that they allow the man to give the woman maximum stimulation of her clitoris.

The basic woman-on-top position is known as the Pair of Tongs Position, in which the woman sits astride her partner facing his head with her knees bent on either side of him. There are many variations of the basic woman-on-top position. She can also sit facing away from her partner, which gives him an exciting view of her buttocks. If she clasps his ankles in this position and then swings herself forwards and backwards, this is known as the Swing Position.

In the Yab Yum position, the man sits cross-legged and the woman sits astride him, with her legs crossed behind his back. The name comes from the Tibetan *yab*, meaning father, and *yum* meaning mother. The position is thought by some to be the ultimate Tantric position for lovemaking and represents the union of male and female principles. It is a very loving and intimate pose.

Rear entry

Rear entry positions allow deep penetration and are particularly appropriate for highly passionate lovemaking. They have animalistic associations, which many people – both men and women – find very arousing.

Rear entry works well in many different positions – lying, standing, sitting or kneeling. Some positions are passionate and abandoned, others are much more relaxed.

One of the more passionate variations is where both partners kneel, the man behind the woman. This position allows deep penetration and leaves the man's hands free to give the woman extra stimulation by stroking her breasts or clitoris.

One of the more relaxed positions is the side-by-side Spoons Position, in which both partners lie on their sides, with knees bent, the man lying behind the woman. This is a cuddly, intimate position, in which it is possible for a couple to make love without actually making any body movements. He has his hands free to stimulate virtually any part of her body. They can simply lie still and quiet, enjoying simply being together, breathing in perfect unison and relishing the feelings in the pelvic region of him being inside her.

Chakras

Whatever position you adopt, you should not become bogged down in the niceties of technique and protocol. There would be little point in this. It is much more important to understand how the posture allows the alignment of your chakras (see page 19) with those of your partner.

It is possible, too, to use postures to create harmonious shapes with your bodies in which energies are generated, channelled and harmonized. Energy can also be circulated between partners by completing the love circuit – usually by joining together certain parts of the body such as the mouths, the tongues or the hands, for example. This will enable you to come closer together emotionally until you both experience a sensation of complete togetherness. The natural culmination of this sensation is – in its extreme form – a feeling of oneness.

Visualizing the energy circuit can also help generate energy. Start, in your mind's eye, with the base chakra and focus inwardly on the energy as it runs up through your seven chakras, to combine eventually with your partner's energy channel at the tops of both your heads.

Maintaining eye contact

Tantric teaching suggests that a couple should look gently into each other's eyes during lovemaking. The result is a sort of sexual meditation, enabling you to direct sex on to a higher focus.

By maintaining intimate and steady eye contact, you should also be able to know what your partner is feeling and when. This will intensify your feelings of closeness.

Breathing

While you are engaging in intercourse – or indeed in any sexual activity – it is important to remember that it is your breathing that connects you to your sexual centre. The deeper you breathe, the greater your contact with your sexual energy. Breathing quietens the mind and engenders an inner silence, which increases awareness and thus allows sensory perceptions to intensify.

Deep breathing will spread far beyond your lungs to your entire body, including your genitals. This enables you to experience your sexual feelings at their most intense and this, in turn, will greatly augment your pleasure and enable you to realize your orgasmic potential.

Pelvic floor muscles

Just as you did when masturbating (see Chapter V), you will continue to benefit if you learn to tense and release your pelvic floor muscles rhythmically in a pumping action while you make love. This applies equally to both men and women. For men, learning to tense and relax these muscles plays the very particular role of helping you to practise semen retention. This is a central tenet in Tantric sex (see page 82), and enables you to prevent ejaculation when you are about to have an orgasm.

For women, tensing these muscles helps to intensify your arousal by improving blood flow. This helps to increase the sensitivity of the whole genital area, including the vagina and clitoris. Squeezing the vaginal area should also give pleasure to your partner.

VIII Orgasm

Men and women experience
orgasm very differently.
It is therefore quite
impossible for men to know
what orgasm feels like for
women, or *vice versa*.
For most of us in the West, orgasm is simply a physical
release. It marks the climax - and therefore the end -
of that particular sexual experience.

This ecstasy doth unperplex
(We said) and tell us what we love,
We see by this it was not sex,
We see, we saw not what did move.
(J. Donne)

But according to the ancient Tantrists, far
from being the end, the orgasm is in fact only
the beginning – the starting point for a deep
and sublime spiritual experience. It represents
a complex shift of powerful kundalini energy
up through the chakras, from the root chakra
at the base of the spine, to the crown chakra
at the top of the head, and thus releases our
spiritual focus.

The ancient Tantrists set great store by
female satisfaction. Female orgasm was, for
them, of the utmost importance, bringing with
it vital, life-giving forces. Men, on the other
hand, should be taught to control their
orgasm so as to be able to make love for
longer periods or repeatedly. There are very
few women who would take objection to this
most basic belief of Tantric thought.

The female orgasm

Ejaculation is not confined to men alone. Many women emit an initial sticky lubricating fluid from the walls of the vagina during arousal. A lot of women then also produce another fluid at the point of orgasm. In addition to this, about one in ten women produce yet another type of fluid, which is a clear, watery liquid and is thought to come from the Skene's glands, which run alongside the urethra. The production of this fluid often makes a woman feel that she is urinating, which, of course, she is not.

In spite of the fact that some women ejaculate, most ancient Tantric texts agree that women – unlike men (see below) – do not lose energy when they reach orgasm. In fact – and quite to the contrary – they actually *gain* energy, by absorbing the male energy.

It is because women do not lose energy at the point of orgasm that masturbation is considered to be more beneficial for them than it is for men. This may explain why pictures of women giving themselves pleasure are much more common in ancient Tantric art than pictures of men.

Women tend to take a lot longer to become aroused than men, and take correspondingly longer to reach the point of climax. Some women actually find it hard to climax, and many find it much easier to climax when masturbating than when making love with a partner – which is one reason why it helps to masturbate in front of a partner and to show him exactly what gives you the greatest pleasure (see page 56).

The female orgasm can range from the mildly pleasurable to the intense and explosive. Different women experience orgasm in different ways, and the same woman can also experience it in different ways according to her mood, her level of energy or fatigue, and her state of health, both physical and emotional.

Different types of female orgasm

Women can experience several different types of orgasm – the clitoral orgasm, the vaginal orgasm, and the G-spot orgasm – each of which feels quite different from the others. It is possible for some women to enjoy all three types simultaneously, though this is by no means common.

It is worth finding out about your orgasms – which type you experience most easily, what causes it, and what it feels like. There are no hard and fast rules and it pays to find out what applies to you.

The clitoris is probably the most sensitive part of a woman's body. In some women, it is so sensitive that they can hardly bear to have it touched, and certainly not at the head, though other women like direct contact and even enjoy quite a rough touch.

A clitoral orgasm occurs as a result of clitoral stimulation, and most women find that this is the easiest type of orgasm to achieve.

The vaginal orgasm, on the other hand, can be quite difficult to achieve, particularly if a woman's lover is insensitive or if his lovemaking is too fast. One way of encouraging the vaginal orgasm is for either you or your partner to stimulate your clitoris and then, when you are about to climax, to change to deep, thrusting penetrative sex. The vaginal orgasm is experienced deeper in the body than the clitoral orgasm, in a series of glorious waves.

The G-spot is a very sensitive area on the front wall of the vagina, about half to two-thirds of the way up. It is named after the man who discovered it, who was a German gynaecologist called Ernest Grafenberg. In certain positions, it may be possible for your partner to stimulate your G-spot, either with his penis or with his fingers. A G-spot orgasm evokes strong feelings of enormous pleasure.

The male orgasm

Orgasm is the penultimate stage of the four stages of a man's sexual cycle. These are:

The arousal stage, when the penis becomes erect.

The plateau phase, when the man continues to be excited, usually for between 15 and 30 minutes.

Orgasm, when the urethra and the deep muscles of the penis simultaneously contract repeatedly and rhythmically, and ejaculation usually occurs.

The refractory phase, during which the penis is flaccid and immediate sexual stimulation does not usually lead to another erection.

For most men, orgasm is the most enjoyable part of sex, the result being that the goal of all sex becomes orgasm. For most Western men, orgasm is usually synonymous with an ejaculatory climax.

This is not, however, the case for Eastern men, who do not perceive ejaculation and orgasm as the same thing. Here, ejaculation is regarded as having only one purpose – that of procreation – while the male orgasm can – and should – be indulged in as often as the man wants.

The ancient Tantrists believed that the semen contains life energy and that it should therefore be retained, and not wasted. Ejaculating was not only a waste of semen, but a waste of energy. The ability to control his ejaculation was therefore seen as one of the most important sexual skills that a man could develop.

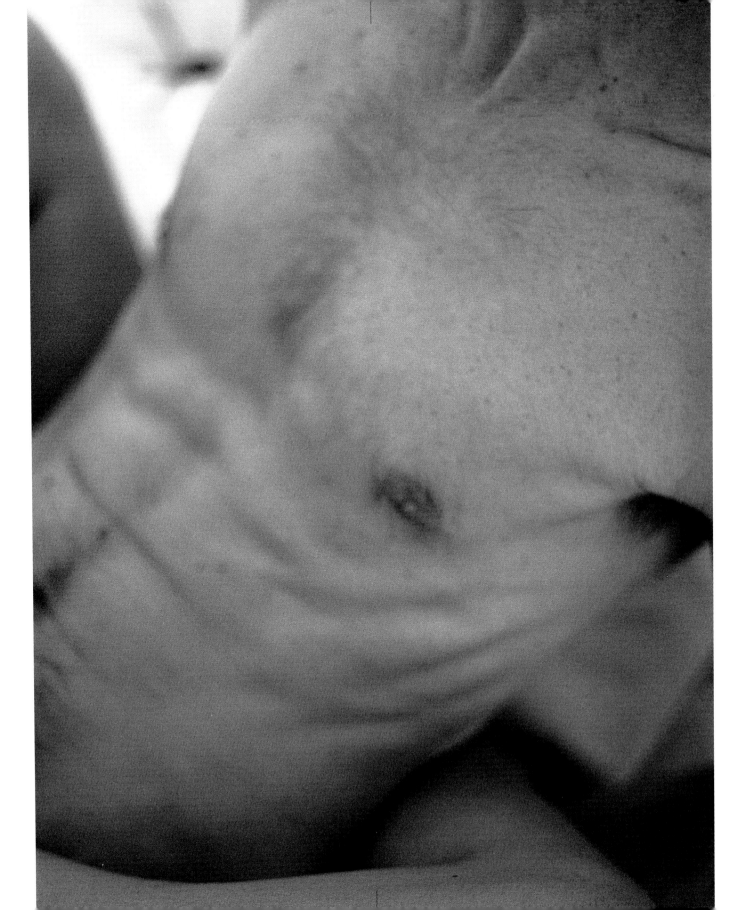

Advantages of not ejaculating

The advantages of the non-ejaculatory, or 'dry' orgasm, impinge on both partners, and are not only physical but psychological, spiritual and emotional.

Many men believe that not to ejaculate must be unhealthy because this interferes with the natural course of the sperm. This is not true, however, and is in fact contrary to Eastern ideas of health and ejaculation. The ancient Tantrists believed that, by practising ejaculation control and retaining his semen, a man will actually be able to conserve his vital life force. This will, in turn, have the effect of prolonging his life, strengthening his body, and helping to promote better health.

It will also intensify his sensitivity and make him more alert to sensations. As a result – and contrary to what many men might expect from a 'dry' orgasm – his orgasms will become 'whole body' orgasms, which are more intense and better than ever.

If a man does not ejaculate, he is also more likely to be able to satisfy his female partner, female sexual satisfaction being of the utmost importance for Tantrists. The reason that so many women in the West experience only clitoral orgasm, as a result of clitoral stimulation, is that most men are not able to have penetrative sex for long periods of time. But if a man can control his ejaculation, he should be able to thrust deeper and longer during penetrative intercourse, which may also help the woman achieve a vaginal orgasm. This is likely to result in a better, more harmonious relationship.

The image of the man who ejaculates and then rolls over, exhausted, to go to sleep has become something of a joke. But there is more than a little truth in the stereotype. Ejaculating *is* exhausting. So it makes sense to concentrate on the best bits of sex, and to leave out the exhausting part.

Lovemaking without ejaculation has no end, and knows no bounds. The man who is able to separate orgasm from ejaculation is able to match the timing of his orgasm with that of his partner. He should also be able to experience multiple orgasms – and, what's even better – he can do this without ejaculation sapping his energy.

Ejaculation control and female satisfaction are both central to Tantric sex. Techniques that a man can employ for controlling his ejaculation and retaining his semen are discussed in more detail in the following chapter.

Whole body orgasm

When he has learned to control his ejaculation, a man can exercise a combination of arousal and relaxation – along with deep and slow breathing – which will enable him to experience a whole body orgasm, rather than a specific, localized genital orgasm.

A whole body orgasm is felt as a continuous series of wavelike thrills, or vibrations. It is more subtle than a genital orgasm, but it is deeper, and it lasts a lot longer. It is not so much a short burst of excitement, or a quick, automatic release, as a slow, conscious act of letting go; not so much an uncontrolled reflex action as a deliberately altered state of consciousness.

IX Prolonging Intercourse

The ability to prolong intercourse requires much practice, patience and dedication. It does not happen easily or automatically, but has to be cultivated and worked at. It takes time. But do not allow yourself to become despondent or discouraged if it does not work first time. The rewards are enormous - for both man and woman alike - so it's well worth the effort.

Now folds the lily all her sweetness up,
And slips into the bosom of the lake:
So fold thyself, my dearest, thou, and slip
Into my bosom and be lost in me.
(A. Lord Tennyson)

Resistance to controlling ejaculation

In the West, men are brought up to believe that ejaculation is the ultimate expression of their sexual power and virility. Young boys may even compete with each other to see who can ejaculate the furthest and highest in order to prove who is the better 'man'.

Women are also brought up to believe the hype. They often think that their partner's ejaculation is proof not only of virility but also of love and affection.

Resistance to the idea of abandoning ejaculation as the be all and end all, and the high point of all sexual experience, may therefore be common in both men and women. But there is nothing magical or mystical about ejaculation. There is not, even, anything particularly 'manly' about it. It is simply an involuntary reflex.

In fact, as mentioned in the last chapter, there are actually many advantages in lovemaking without ejaculating (see page 84), including:

• Higher energy levels.
• A longer and healthier life.
• More fulfilling sex for the woman.
• A more harmonious relationship.
• Better orgasms for both of you.

Controlling ejaculation

Controlling ejaculation is about much more than merely *stopping* ejaculation. It is also about a man redirecting his sexual energy, or *ching*, and circulating it within his own body, and from there to his partner. The result is a complete energy circuit, whereby both partners experience the oneness of perfect harmony and balance.

A man's ability to control ejaculation requires both understanding and cooperation on his partner's part. This is particularly true where penetrative sex is concerned.

He will also need to understand his own personal sexual rhythms. He should be familiar with how fast – or how slowly – he is able to reach orgasm. He should understand, too, which positions are more or less conducive to orgasm.

How to do it

There are a number of different methods that you can use to help control your ejaculation. The different methods described here can be used either singly or in unison, depending on what you find works best for you.

One of the simplest things you can do which can help delay ejaculation is to stay completely still, relaxing both the genital and anal muscles, and meanwhile to press your tongue against the roof of your mouth about 1cm (¹/₂ inch) or so behind your front teeth where the palate curves down. This creates a feeling of being anchored, which can itself assist in postponing ejaculation, and also helps direct the kundalini energy down the front of the body and back down to the base chakra, where it belongs. The Tantrists speak of the energy becoming stuck if this is not done.

Another simple way is to take deep, regular breaths. These will slow your heart rate, which, in turn, will calm things down and will delay any pressing need to ejaculate.

Another method of stopping your ejaculation, when you feel that you are reaching the point of no return and ejaculation is imminent, is to withdraw your penis a little from your partner's vagina – say, by 2.5cm (1 inch) or so. When you feel that your need to climax is subsiding, you can start thrusting deeper again. One way of doing this is to follow the Tantric principle of Sets of Nine: this involves alternating nine shallow thrusts with a single deep one.

If you find that nine thrusts in succession like this are too arousing, try just three thrusts and then gradually build up to nine. If shallow thrusting doesn't work for you, you could try withdrawing your penis altogether until you feel able to resume without climaxing. In the meantime, continue stimulating your partner with your fingers so that she does not feel left out.

Yet another way of preventing ejaculation and one favoured in Tantric teaching is to press the index and middle fingers of one hand (or the index finger and thumb, as you prefer) against a particular point on your perineum, midway between your anus and your scrotum. Either you or your partner can do this, depending on what position you are in and which is easier.

The effect of this technique is to stop semen leaving the prostate and entering the urethra, in preparation for ejaculation. Instead, it stays in the prostate, where it is reabsorbed into the bloodstream and circulated to the rest of the body. This technique may well make you lose your erection, but this should not present a problem: simply put your now soft penis back in her vagina, where you should find it surprisingly easy to get an erection again.

Finally, yet another method for preventing ejaculation is what is known as the Squeeze technique, which was originally developed for men who suffer from a tendency to ejaculate prematurely.

This is a more modern technique, evolved by sexologists Masters and Johnson, which involves placing the thumb on the frenulum, on the underside of the penis, with the index and middle fingers on the ridge of the glans on its upper side, and squeezing for between 10 and 15 seconds, or until the urge to ejaculate has passed. Again, this can be done either by the man or by the woman, and again, you will probably lose your erection.

Afterplay

However expert you become at extending intercourse, and for however long you are able to prolong the experience, all good things come to an end. There will therefore inevitably come a time when it will eventually stop.

Even then, however, things are not completely finished. Or, at least, they ought not to be, and for many people, afterplay is almost as important as foreplay.

This applies in particular to women, many of whom experience feelings of anti-climax and disappointment when their male partner has finished making love and simply rolls over and goes to sleep or, worse still, gets up and turns on the telly or takes a shower.

The time after making love is a special time. It is for gentle and loving feelings of togetherness. A couple should stay close for a while after lovemaking and enjoy each other in a state of complete relaxation. Express your feelings, and tell each other you love one another. Above all, give yourself time to savour the moment. This is a precious time. Do not waste it.

Glossary

asana A yoga posture.

chakras Energy centres in the body, from the Sanskrit word for wheels.

ching Taoist term for sexual energy.

Hinduism Religion originating in northern India some 4,000 years ago.

kundalini The powerful latent energy, usually depicted as a coiled serpent, that resides in the base chakra.

lingam The penis, often represented as an emblem of Shiva.

maithuna Sexual union.

mantra A word or phrase that is repeated a number of times, either silently or aloud, as an aid to transcendental meditation.

meditation Act of spiritual contemplation. A central practice in Tantra, and in Tantric sex.

meridians A complex system of invisible pathways throughout the body, through which energy is said to run.

moksha A term for the female orgasm.

pranayama A branch of yoga that is associated with breathing exercises

Sanskrit The ancient written language of the Hindu scriptures.

Shakti The Supreme Goddess and legendary consort of Shiva.

Shiva The Supreme Being and legendary consort of the goddess Shakti.

Tantra A form of Hinduism and Buddhism which emphasizes the division of the universe into male and female forces that maintain its unity by their interaction. It is associated with magical and sexual practices that imitate the union of Shiva and Shakti, as described in religious books called the Tantras.

Taoism An ancient system of belief which originated in China.

Yang The Cosmic Masculine, according to Taoism. It is the constant interplay of Yin and Yang that makes up the entire universe. See also Yin.

Yin The Cosmic Feminine, according to Taoism. It is the constant interplay of Yin and Yang that makes up the entire universe. See also Yang.

yoga A system of physical postures to promote well-being, both physical and mental. Yoga is a Sanskrit word meaning 'union' or 'joining', referring to the union of the individual with the deepest level of consciousness, which this physical discipline is said to make possible.

yoni The vulva, often represented as an emblem of Shakti.

Index

Useful Addresses

Zek and Misha Halu's
Sacred Sexuality
PO Box 1002
London SE23 3QJ
Tel: 0181 699 2066
(locations in London,
Rome, Arozona, Skyros,
Israel, Czech Republic)

Skyros
92 Prince of Wales Rd
London NW5 3NE
Tel: 0171 267 4424

Patrick Keeley's Taoist
Sexual Training
PO Box 3548
London
NW6 6RT
Tel: 0171 624 7267

Margo Anand's Skydancing
Institutes
20 Sunnyside Avenue
Suite A219
Mill Valley
CA 94941
Tel: 415 927 2584

John Hawken
Skydancing Institute UK
Lower Grumbola Farm
Newbridge
Penzance
Cornwall
TR20 8QZ
Tel: 01736 788304

Wild Dance Events
15 Quadrant Grove
London
NW5 4JT
Tel: 0171 813 4260

Acknowledgements

Publishing Director
Laura Bamford

Commissioning Editor
Jane McIntosh
Assistant Editor
Catharine Davey

Art Director
Keith Martin
Executive Art Editor
Mark Winwood

Photography
Salvatore

Production Controller
Dawn Mitchell

*The publishers wish to thank the following
organizations for their kind permission to
reproduce the photographs in this book:
Bridgeman Art LIbrary/British Library p 12
E. T. Archive/British Museum p 13*

*The publishers would like to thank the following:
Models Lucy Latimer and Leigh Tolson
(in training with Skydancing UK)
Joe's Basement
(for the provision of Scala and Polaroid film)*